Like Silencing the Wind

poems by

Pearl Karrer

Finishing Line Press
Georgetown, Kentucky

Like Silencing the Wind

for my family,

near & far

Copyright © 2024 by Pearl Karrer
ISBN 979-8-88838-673-6 First Edition
All rights reserved under International and Pan-American Copyright Conventions. No part of this book may be reproduced in any manner whatsoever without written permission from the publisher, except in the case of brief quotations embodied in critical articles and reviews.

ACKNOWLEDGMENTS

Grateful acknowledgment is made to the following publications in which these poems first appeared:

CALIFORNIA QUARTERLY: "A Vet With One Leg," "Gulf"
COFFEE & CHICORY: "Printmaking: Etching A Zinc Plate with Nitric Acid Bites"
DOS PASSOS REVIEW: "Plitvička"
IBIS REVIEW: "*Memory*"
PENUMBRA: "Like Silencing the Wind"
RED WHEELBARROW: "Cork Oak"
SLANT: "Croatia: #120, Highway 42, Remembers," "*She Who Was Once the Helmet-Maker's Beautiful Wife*," "The Leather Shoe"
THE COMSTOCK REVIEW: "Croatia: #125, Highway 42," "Henrietta"
THE LUCID STONE: "Pfefferberg Gasthaus Room Four"
VISIONS-International: "Near Chichen Itza"
WATERWOOD PRESS ANTHOLOGY: NO, ACHILLES: "South of Vrobovsko"

Publisher: Leah Huete de Maines
Editor: Christen Kincaid
Cover Art: Pearl Karrer
Author Photo: John Hoch
Cover Design: Stephanie Bloom Pressman, Frog on the Moon Press

Order online: www.finishinglinepress.com
also available on amazon.com

Author inquiries and mail orders:
Finishing Line Press
PO Box 1626
Georgetown, Kentucky 40324
USA

Contents

She Who Was Once the Helmet-Maker's Beautiful Wife ... 1
The Wool Wagon ... 2
Anderson Ranch Wool Wagon, Photograph c. 1913 ... 3
Henrietta ... 4
Henrietta, Photograph c. 1915, Butte, Montana ... 5
Summer Solstice, June 6, 1944 ... 6
Pfefferberg Gasthaus, *Room Four* ... 7
Printmaking: Etching a Zinc Plate with Nitric Acid Bites ... 8
Cork Oak ... 9
A Vet with One Leg ... 10
Plitvička ... 11
Plitvička National Park, Photograph ... 12
Wishing, Monotype ... 13
Croatia: #125, Highway 42 ... 14
Croatia: # 120, Highway 42 Remembers ... 15
South of Vrbovsko ... 16
The Leather Shoe ... 17
Boston Marathon ... 19
Blackberry-Time ... 20
Near Chichen Itza ... 21
Temple to Mayan Sun God, Photograph ... 22
Venus, in her place, ... 23
Gulf ... 24
Indigo Variations ... 25
Lost Voices: Maksym Kryvtsov ... 26
Memory ... 28
Memory, Mixed Media, 30" x 24" ... 29
Like Silencing the Wind ... 30

She Who Was Once the Helmet-Maker's Beautiful Wife

draws me to her niche each time I
enter the Rodin collection. Braids lock
her hair in an arc to the nape of her neck.
Their bronze patina masks
gray strands. I see past

to a girl with auburn waves
held back with a ribbon. She has no
idea she will marry a helmet-maker,
that the breasts beginning to nub
under her pinafore will grow hot and hard
with lactation, will eventually

sag onto this rough pedestal. Her ears
no longer ring with the blows of metal
on metal, the hoof beats of cavalry
serving Napoleon. She sits, one hand
behind her back, not trying to hide

gaunt bones of her shoulders,
trough of her spine, her stomach—
distended   Head
bowed, the set of her chin hints

at resilience. To have been so placed
on this pedestal! I stand
on the tile floor, unnoticed—
one of several viewing the collection.
Gray streaks my long braid; creases
furrow my neck. My breasts
begin their downward slide.

Note:
Auguste Rodin,
Celle Qui Fut La Belle Heaulmière,
1887, bronze, height 19 inches.

The Wool Wagon
Photograph, c. 1913, Butte, Montana

Burlap bulges with wool, the shorn
wealth of his ranch, rising
in sacks three layers high, stretched
across the bed of the wagon—

first stage of their transformation
from fleece on free range sheep
to uniforms and blankets warming
troops on battlefields in France.

My grandfather sits on the wool sacks—
second tier. A pair of black horses
whinny in their traces
behind a pinto and bay.

Silver studs accent their bridles.
Holding the reigns, my grandfather
presses his foot on a lever.
The brake shoes retract. Wooden rims

creak forward with a progressive rise
and fall of mottled spokes. Sun and wind
furrow his face; a black mustache
monitors his moods. Turning,

he smiles at his young son and daughter.
Astride the top sacks, they
urge on the horses. Bows
butterfly above their blond curls.

They bounce in high-bib overalls.
Cousin Della and Aunt Henrietta
perch within arm's reach, pinafores
fluttering over the burlap.

Beneath them the great wheels groove
parallel tracks in the rock-knobbed earth, up
an incline past barn, gnarled apple, sapling
pens to hold lambs. The weight of wool

anchors each sack; the corners
of the top seams twitch like ears.
Black capitals, **A. E. ANDERSON**, stamp
my grandfather into each burlap flank.

Anderson Ranch Wool Wagon, Photograph c. 1913

Henrietta
Photograph, c. 1915, Butte, Montana

Her face, a pale oval, tilts
to one side under the regulation
army hat. Chestnut hair scallops
shadow across her forehead.
Longer strands hide in a twist
pinned at the back of her head.

A smile teases
her lips while she stares
at the camera with the confidence
of youth, health and the Army's
crash course in nursing.

Wounded, waking
under this gaze, will return
to her years later—pilgrims
bearing tokens of faith,
like the howitzer casing, its brass
stamped with an eagle
clutching a cross.

A white collar peeps
above the heavy wool jacket.
On one lapel, brass snakes
twine a winged hope
beside the letters U and S.

The glove on her left hand
swells over her ring;
these fingers have not yet
held the telegram
regretting his loss.

Her long skirt fades from the sepia
onto a field in France.

Henrietta, Photograph c. 1915, Butte, Montana

Summer Solstice, June 6, 1944

Perched on a kitchen chair
I want to wriggle
free from grandmother's fingers
tightly locking my corn silk strands
into French pigtails, cry out
with each pull and tug.
Braids tied off, I escape
in search of my playmates.

Walnut branches shake
under our weight as we climb
high in the canopy.
Hidden by leaves, we track
Mike and Boomer. They
enter the rear alley, stirring up dust—
closer—closer. Fusillades of nuts,
tracer bullets, shoot up spurts
of warm dirt. Boomer barks,
racing to retrieve; Mike lobs
them back, then swings up
to join the ambush.

He boasts, *A letter from France!*
His brother—remember the day
he left? His khaki uniform?
His easy grin?
He swung us in flying circles.

We plan for the Matinee
this Saturday—ten cents to see
The Perils of Pauline
plus Black &White scenes
from battlefields in France.
Will Mike's brother be in them?

Scrambling down from the walnut,
I yelp with pain. Blood
spills from a gash down my leg—

Pfefferberg Gaustaus
      Room Four

Acorns hurl against the grate
beneath his window, strafing

sleep—staccato
voices in the strasse.

Another war
peering through low branches—

a tall boy gleans
the cratered field;

he shifts a rifle, unstraps
canteen and helmet. A coat

swallows his thin body, strong
with sweat despite the frost.

His stomach whines.
Wind-borne slaps of steel

drive him up the oak,
this high limb, one leg

dangling—he
jerks with each volley

under the eiderdown, gray
hair drenched and matted.

Printmaking: Etching A Zinc Plate With Nitric Acid Bites

Asphaltum floods the plate; my needle
cuts to explore the strengths of her face.

> a kick whiplashes
> our door   backgammon men
> grind under boots   rifles
> prod my father and brother
> outside on the snow
> no jackets   no shoes   all
> the men of our village
> betrayed in the square
>
> mother grabs
> blankets   we reach
> the shed   the bare
> poplars   flames
> snap our wood
> houses   shots

My needle stipples resistance
into her pores, wrinkles her skin.

> poplars flick
> yellow against concrete
> houses   in the square
> boys with black curly hair
> kick a soccer ball
> past German tourists
> near the carved granite I clip
> blood red roses   my black
> dress one more shadow

Cork Oak

Oak, have you heard?
They are coming.
They smell of vino tinto,
cebollas, salchichon.

Do you see the soil,
brick-colored and warm
spiraling dust like powdered
bone with each footfall?

Does the earth tremble
its warning, a vibration
unlike the rooting of boars?

Does the sudden
absence of talons,
of song in your canopy
scare you?

Lift up your limbs
in supplication—
they are coming.
Lift up your limbs—
they are here.

How do you bear
the slice of sharp steel?
Your bark ripped
off in wide swatches,
trunk red and bleeding?

A Vet with One Leg

presses into view manipulating
metal crutches down the right
side of University Avenue.
Between sweeps of my windshield
blades he looks back,
often, over his left shoulder—four
lanes of traffic, pulsing,
held in check by the light
bleeding into the intersection.

He ignores the rain.
His black hair mats. His short
jacket sticks to his back.

As he nears the south entrance
to Bayshore Freeway I tense, the light
ready to change. Instead of crossing
to the next segment of sidewalk,
he follows the on-ramp past the no
hitchhiking warning. My lane

spurts ahead—not his
direction, yet I carry
the flash of his crutches,
dripping with rain, the hollow
of his Jeans right leg, rolled up
and pinned against my torso.

Plitvička

Lake cascades
into lake, slips
over the travertine lips
    (like the policeman falling)
of aqua pools or
plunges down a limestone
escarpment,
    (like the policeman falling)
misting moss and ferns.
Everywhere, the tympani
of water, the Plitvička River
descending through karst
landscape—
    (like the policeman falling)
sixteen lakes,
beech-fir forests.
Boardwalks edge
rushing water, cross
shallow lakes, planks
slick with spray.
Trout, brown bear,
thrush and dragonfly
claim their niche
like the fringe
of white washed villages
unprepared
Easter 1991,
Serbian bullets,
    Josip Jović,
        park policeman,
            falling—

Note:
Croatia's first National Park, 1949.
Shots fired there initiated
the 1990s Serbo-Croatian war.

Plitvička National Park, Photograph May 8, 2009

Wishing, Monotype, 30" x 24"
Pearl Karrer

Croatia: #125, Highway 42

Shells ricochet from my second story,
punch holes in the stucco.
Chimney bricks pitch
down the steep metal roof.
Explosions shatter my balcony—
the one with wrought-iron
daisies, where my mistress loved
to gossip with neighbors.

In my nightmares I hear them coming,
just after midnight, no moon, clouds
shrouding the sky. Gunfire—my neighbors'
voices—shouts to my master—
come out, Croat, bring your family!

He sends them scrambling
through the back bedroom window,
the yew hedge, the black knob of hill,
into the forest beyond. Upstairs he
crouches from window to window, firing
his dad's old rifle, running out of shells.

Years pass without familiar footsteps,
children's laughter, song fests
with guitar and mandolin,
My kitchen, cold. Spices, baking
bread, no longer scent the air. Shades
darken the upper rooms; paint
sloughs in tan patches; moss
and lichens scab the stucco.
Along the highway, with each
passing car, unpruned roses
flail the air with whip-like canes.

Croatia: #120, Highway 42, Remembers

April is the cruellest month...
The Waste Land, T. S. Eliot

April, 1941—my master's wife
hanging clothes in the back yard,
apple blossoms in her hair.
They came—Ustaše officers in Nazi
uniforms—my Serb family, forced
into a truck—one son, overlooked,
picking mushrooms among the firs.

April, 1950—he returns to claim me,
builds a second story. The walls
welcome laughter, crayon drawings.
Children climb the apple tree.
Evenings after Schnapps, sometimes tears,
tales of his parents, sisters, Ustaše banner
disappearing down the road.

April, 1990—loud voices, worries
crowd my rooms. Franjo Tuđman's
election brings back Ustaše symbols—
uniforms, checkered flag, kuna
currency—they stoke my family's fears.

April, 1991—radios blare
news from Plitvička National Park—
park policeman in the Ustaše uniform,
killled by Serb irregulars. My family
gathers relatives—oil
weapons on the kitchen table.

April, 2009—a new couple climbs
my stairs—fresh stucco seals
bullet holes, anchors repaired windows.
How long will this last?
My upstairs dormers look down on
the gnarled apple's fragile bloom.

South of Vrbovsko

Highway 42 winds
two lanes southeast
through Croatia—
low hills, stippled
with lime colored beech,
spikes of dark fir.
Rural villages
give way to fallow fields;
mid-May, yet wild grass
instead of grain.
No cattle graze.
A small boy,
emerging from a barn,
chases his dog; a cap
dangles from its mouth.
The spaniel prances
to a wire fence and slips
through a gap
into the pasture.
Shouting, the boy
follows. There are no signs
warning—*Mine Fields*—
still no funds to clear
them all away. Twenty
years and more—ticking—

The Leather Shoe

1.
She rubs flax oil
into the cowhide shoes,
shaped to fit
her small feet;
stuffs wild grasses
into the hollows,
laces leather thongs
through the paired eyelets—
sure to be walking
in them again
after the danger passes.

Finding a pit
in the back of the cave,
she places her treasure
under a pottery bowl,
adds a cushion of leaves.

The Armenian cave
shelters gravesites,
sheep during storms.
In the valley below,
mudbrick pisé dwellings
transition—stone houses,
cement villages,
electric lit cities—
the Copper Age cedes
to the passing millennia.

2.
My newspaper headlines:
Copper Age couture
with a picture captioned—
world's oldest known leather shoe—
found in cave Areni-1,
preserved by a strata

of sheep dung.
Intrigued, I take two
heavy bookends from a shelf,

wipe dust from a pair of bronzed
shoes. Their copper patina
glows; the eyelets,
laced and tied with a bow.
Once a soft white leather—
my first steps
held on an onyx base.

Replacing them in the bookcase,
I wonder, will they last
five millennia?
Will archeologists
digging in a Palo Alto tel,
surmise their use, the books,
missing long ago?

Boston Marathon
    April 15, 2013

Cheers urge the runners on.
    Fans line sidewalks,
        crowd the finish line—

Two blasts rip, flatten—
    acrid smoke, panic,
        strewn hats, packs, shoes—

Blood spills across
    shattered Boylston Street,
        screaming fans—

A runner wakes up to pain,
    triage hands, tourniquets,
        his missing leg—

Note:
April 15 celebrates Patriot's Day,
first battles of the American Revolution.

Blackberry-Time

Armed with a long barbeque tong
and aluminum pan, I enter

>Blackberry-Time—relinquish today.
>Threats of jihadists, pandemics,
>unemployment shrink
>to this jumble of thorns.
>I accept their protection, ignore
>sharp jabs from hidden barbs
>
>Lifting a cane, my bare arm slips
>into dappled space; berries
>dangle almost within reach.
>The black wink
>in each green and red cluster
>draws me into the patch.
>My fingers soon stain
>bright crimson.
>
>The scent of warm berries
>wafts around me like wine—
>Zinfandel, Pinot Noir.
>My pan heaps again and again.
>Fresh blackberry cobbler
>tonight, jam tomorrow.

Each winter spoonful,
a return to this haven,
this Blackberry-Time.

Near Chichen Itza

Have you ever walked as the sun
dipped low in the west
backlighting a derelict building—

> Mine was limestone, crusted
> with lichen, a colonial church,
> three bell towers on a low knoll.

and ventured to peer past boards
on windows, moved along paving
fragmented by bracken and grass,
stopped at an open doorway,
tempted to step over the threshold?

> Dampness permeated this room,
> the back half in deep shadow,
> pallet of dirty rags, empty cans,
> eggshells, machete—
> A fresh smell of rancid sweat
> stung my nostrils—I fled
> to the dusty road feeding
> taxis to a Mayan god.

Have you ever relaxed in a courtyard,
cold drink in hand, watching the full moon
crest a tile roof, float across a pool
creating two apricot spheres so bright
you could read, but you listened
instead to the pulsing crescendo of frogs,
kitchen clatter and laughter?

> Yucatan pibil came fragrant with spice,
> dorado fresh from the sea. A feast

compared to the derelict room;
its memories crowded into my courtyard,
found a seat at my table, fingered
silver and stemware.
Around us, limestone walls
bone-white in the moonlight.

Temple to Mayan Sun God, Photograph

Venus, in her place,

a three quarters moon
soft glowing, the sky,
still flush with twilight;
the salivating scents
of sautéed garlic,
cinnamon and citrus oil,
lamp-lit kitchens,
open to the night.
The sidewalk, empty
under its canopy of branches,
the sycamores releasing
their first leaves of fall.
They scuff against my shoes,
crunch like brittle paper.
My senses register
a place at peace,
yet images from Syria
crowd in—gassed children
follow, trailing
long white shrouds.

Gulf

Vocalized—the G
gags, the F hisses.
Viewed—it pulses in waves
against the lip of land,
lulls with cyclic rhythm.

Travelers flood beaches
backed by luxury high-rise:
*utsukushii, molto bella,
c'est bonne, is gut—*

South of Cancún
remnants of jungle
nudge sand coves.
Coconut fronds scrape,
insects drone. Hammocks
sway under thatch palapas;
natives close their eyes—
their single low table,
three stone cooking place,
earthen floor

give way to pyramids—
ancient limestone
thrust above ceiba
and chicle trees. Venus
glows through her portal.
Mayan chants climb
steep stairs to Iqi-Balam,
Jaguar of the Moon,
to Húracán, Heart of the Sky.

Indigo Variations

1.
Astride his camel,
a Taureg nomad
races a sandstorm
across the Sahara.
Hand-dyed wool
turbans his head,
cocoons his face,
tunics his body.
The fabric's indigo
seeps into his pores.
In battle, his blue skin
terrifies the enemy.

2.
From the leather thong
around his neck, a Blue Eye
dangles. The charm's
circle of thick cobalt glass
features a central white lens,
turquoise rim, blue-black iris.
In his Turkish village, Blue Eyes
glare from the tops of doorways,
peer through windows, reflect
evil wishes back to the sender.

3.
Plantations take root
in New World colonies—indigo,
cotton, rice. Fearing evil spirits,
Africans, brought in to work the fields,
protect their quarters with Haint Blue
paint—*Indigofera* dye,
buttermilk and lye. Brushed
on the frames of windows and doors,
it mimics the water *haints* cannot cross.

Lost Voices, Maksym Kryvtsov
January 22, 1990-January 7, 2024,
Russian invasion of Ukraine

Hoarfrost clings to his mustache & beard.
He scans the shell cratered terrain
around the trench and dugout he calls *home*.
No enemy alerts so far on his smartphone.
Whistling shrill calls, he sees his orange tabby
emerge from a copse of trees.

They settle in the dugout, the cat cleaning mud,
bits of vole fur from his white paws. Maksym
opens a dried ration, remembers warm meals,
Kyiv's bustle before Russia invaded. Then he had
his National University degree, the routine
of work, baking a cheesecake for friends,
visits to family in Rivne, Even a collection
of poetry, winning a PEN Ukraine Award—
Virshi z biinytsi, (Poems from the Embrasure).

He pulls out his notebook and pen, opens
Facebook to post to his followers. Lately, Death
has crept into his poem. Watching his sleeping cat
stretch, he writes—*My Ginger Tabby...*
dreams of an unscathed brick house/
dreams of chickens/....
my helmet slips out of my hands/
falls on the mud/...

In another, *True Propaganda*, he asks,
Where are my dreams?../Look!
They are hiding in trenches/
We are returning from the mission/
Exhausted and empty/....

January 5th he posts, *My bones/*
Will sink into the earth/...
My spare clothes and equipment/
Will be given to new recruits/...
To finally
          Bloom
                As a violet.

Two days later, soldiers find Maksym,
his ginger cat, inside the shelled
ruins of his dugout. Kyiv's
St. Michael's Golden-Domed Monastery
fills with mourners two weeks
before his 33rd birthday. They continue
his farewell on Maidan Square, carrying
poems
          photos
                  bunches of violets.

Note:
He is buried on the Alley of Heroes,
Nove Cemetary, Rivne, Ukraine

Memory
Mixed Media, (30"x24")

hangs above my computer
juxtaposing chips
and megabytes with a man
in a turban. His Afghan robe
contours crossed legs, knees
knobbing at right angles as he
sits on a rug in his desert
encampment. We share
no name yet eyes down-
cast he radiates the posture
of my son absorbed in a book.
My father's cheekbones and nose
haunt the strong face.
Left hand on left knee,
his long fingers splay
as if on the frets
of my husband's guitar.
Tea steams from the cup
in his right hand.
Before him a woman
moves in his reverie.
Tendrils of smoke
part to reveal her face.
Her lips forgive,
carrying my daughter's smile
to her cheeks. Her eyes
tend the fire she
stirs with a stick.
Below them, the black
void of a photogram
where exposed whites
and grays rise to the surface—
a ring of firing pins for a pistol
brought back from Kabul,
the tines of a fork,
sand glittering like eyes.

Ribbons of peeled cucumber
curve into Islamic
calligraphy. The glyphs
soar and twist.

Memory, Mixed Media, 30" x 24"
Pearl Karrer

Like Silencing the Wind
    for Sushmita Banerje

Just the age of my daughter,
Sushmita, dragged from her Afghan
home; 1:30 a.m., her husband,
blindfolded and bound,
their shattered door,
open to the wind.

An Islamic madrassa,
near al-Jihad,
witnessed the fifteen bullets
ending forty-five years,
her aid to others.

Brave enough
to marry an Afghan
against her family's wishes;
convert from Hindu to Islam;
write about life
under Taliban control.

Her book, *A Kabuliwala's
Bengalli Wife*, 1989,
retold in 2003—
the Indian film,
Escape from Taliban.

    Women—
    forced to wear burkas,
    not work, nor leave home
    without a male escort.
    School, forbidden
    to a girl.

Her medical dispensary,
closed by the Taliban.
      Imprisoned
      in a mud brick hut,
she tunnels free,
escapes to India.

Safe, after twenty years,
she rejoins her husband.

The notice of her murder,
September 6th, 2013,
carries no banner headlines,
no wake-up calls
against the agents of her death.

Yet, continents apart,
isn't that her voice
in the wind
outside our windows?

From a log cabin in a Montana mining camp to her present home in Palo Alto, California, **Pearl Karrer** travels extensively. After a degree in microbiology from Cornell University, leading to cancer research, she currently teaches piano, exhibits art in juried shows and writes poetry. Her monotypes have been in exhibitions like the biennial printmaking shows, *Pacific Rim*, University of Hawaii, Hilo; the traveling *Monotype Forum*, ending at the University of California, Davis. Her poems appear in such journals as the *Cider Press Review, Spillway, Whetstone* and 10 anthologies. Her poetry collection, *Weathering*, won a Hudson Valley Writer's Center Competition, judged by Denise Levertov. *The Thorn Fence*, set in Tanzania and Kenya, and *Balanced Between Water and Sky*, set in the Florida Everglades, both explore the boundaries between people and nature (Finishing Line Press). She has retired from editing the *California State Poetry Quarterly*.

www.ingramcontent.com/pod-product-compliance
Lightning Source LLC
Chambersburg PA
CBHW040308170426
43194CB00022B/2939